The poems in this volume were composed in one of the nation's largest mental hospitals. Some of them were written outside of conscious awareness, and some during more settled periods; which may explain any apparent repetition and also the slight confusion in, for example, "Unrealities." May I make it clear that the descriptions of the various types of patients, and also of the different therapies, are written purely from my own observations and impressions, with no pretense to any clinical knowledge.

Much appreciation for their help and interest is due to Mrs. M. G., to A. K. of the American Red Cross and her helpers on the staff of the Hospital's newspaper, to the students who typed and assembled this material, and to my fellow-patients who first inspired me to collect these verses in book form.

EITHNE TABOR
Spring, 1950

THE
Cliff's Edge

songs of a psychotic

by Eithne Tabor

SHEED & WARD
New York

CONTENTS

PRELUDE

WARNING

The neat-piled sheaves of the garnered skills
And the golden grains of learning—
Scattered they lie like a field of wheat
Destroyed by the winds of yearning.
Bitter the taste of the bread turned stone,
Of the clear air clogged with ashes—
Bitter and cold are the wind and rain;
And the sword that the lightning flashes
Is cruel and keen. O'er the cliff's sheer edge
I am reeling, plunging, falling,
And out on the hidden seas beyond,
A vanished voice is calling,
For the sound of the past in my deafened ears
Is a lone lost seagull's crying;
While my manacled soul, which the gods struck down,
Like Prometheus of old, lies dying . . .

SEARCH

Dark is the forest
Faint the trail,
And weary unto death am I—
Lonely as is the unfriended hawk
Circling the grey and empty sky . . .
Ah, little lostling
Of my heart—
Can you hear, and can you hear?
And have you looked
Into those eyes—
The cold, green-glowing eyes
Of Fear?
And can you hear?
And can you hear?

LOOM

This is the frame, hand-hewn, erect and square;
(Treadles and pegs and bars, — all these
Are fair simplicity.)

This is the shuttle; this, the levelling-comb;
(More complex now, the shapes carven
And smoothed to usefulness.)

And these, the warp and weft . . . the spun, dyed threads,
Some pegged taut, others loosely wrapped
Upon the shuttle's blade . . .

(So simple-seeming, yet so vastly changed
From their first selves into what now
Follows the weaver's hands!)

Know these the weaver's will? O tangled thread!
Wove I this shred of cloth, so weak
So patternless; and did

My fingers make these beauty-strangling knots?
Loom of my life, the truth is there . . .
Too confident of skill

Where no skill lay, too hasty were these hands.
Now, the relentless shears rend. Ah!
Sorrow is keen of blade.

WILDERNESS PEAK

Above,
The wild-eyed stars
Glare from the wasteland of infinity,
The wind
Runs its unceasing search-course—
Pitiful
Its sobbing in the blasted skeleton pines.
Head low—
Face hidden in fear, clouds scud the sky . . .

Darkness
Without end, mantles the moon.

Below—
Aye, far below—
Lights in the valley
Twinkle—ah! Pin-points of security!
So small, so helpless in fragility!
Mists

Lie like a strangling rope
Round the mountain's throat,
Flow in a silent flood,
Cold-fingered, through the warm hills.
Silence
Pregnant with sound—muteness of fear . . .

Afar—
Black waves, still deeps—
Gaunt cliffs—
Silver shale—
Foam crawling—and the sound of the sea . . .

Eternity . . . .

No going back . . .
Hush—do not speak—
This is the peak . . . . . .

BREAKDOWN

This is how it starts . . .
Some thing you knew or once had known—
Some beast deep-kennelled in your soul
Bays at the moon—
Leaps the full length of its chain;
And falls back beaten.
The thing is done—you carry on.

This is how it goes on . . .
The struggle waxes
Till night and day are filled
With that wild hideous howling;
And control
Is slipping, slipping—
Is nearly gone—still, you go on.

This is how it ends . . .
The weak link snaps at last.
The wild thing freed
Leaps at your guardless throat . . .
You wake up beating
At a padlocked door.
There is no more.

CASE HISTORY

It is so simple and so bare.
First it was there
In all its tangibility—
And now, for me
It has no shape, nor form, nor entity.
And is it I
Or someone else—
And did I do it yesterday
Or now—or is it in futurity?
And is this what you mean by insecurity?
I am ashamed—why guilt?
Why was that coffee spilt?
I'll see a doctor soon—my nerves are shot.
Psychiatrist? A lot of tommyrot.
Well, doctor . . . Oh my God! Nurse, where am I?
A mental institution? God, but why?
A nervous breakdown—why that's simply plain—
Dear God in Heaven—am I then
Insane?

And with what silence
And what song
And with what tears

And with what laughter
And what hopes
And with what fears

And with what labour
Not of hands
But broken hearts

And with what woundings
By what arrows
And what darts

By what grey banks
And swampy shallows
Of what streams

Deep running, dark-depth'd,
Were you built
Prison of lost dreams?

MENTAL CASE

Nay, do not cast a stone.
Though she is fettered, she has done no wrong
As we would see it.
A prisoner? Perhaps—
But not the way
You think—she is her own severest jailer.
And do not pity her—she is beyond tears—
And do not laugh, for fear and hate and pain
Are not meet subjects for a comedy.
Who is she?
That is hard to say.
She's not herself—nor you—nor me—
Nor anyone outside whom we may know.
A person? No . . . Now, just a number.
Oh!

CO-MATES IN EXILE

SCHIZOPHRENIA

O thou twin-blossoming rose!
What seed of the unreal produced thee?
And what the fatal germ
Sending thy roots, thy reaching, rambling stem,
On the strange twisted path of this thy life?
Aye, 'mongst thine interfolded petals
Ere they had burst to bloom,
The golden heart already blasted lay.

Before the sun had crimsoned thee, thou hadst borne
Ah, not a lovely flower—but a thorn.

CATATONIA

Is it past believing?
Leaving, leaving . . .
Weaving downward . . .
Blurred . . .
No word.

Is it now true-seeming?
Dreaming, dreaming—
Screaming
Voiceless—
Unheard—
No word.

Is it then eye-seeing?
Fleeing, fleeing—
Conflicts—
Erred—
No word.

Is't past understanding?
Standing, standing—
Demanding—
Something
Deeply stirred—
No word.

PARANOID

Legions against him,
None to aid—
Somewhere there's plotting—
A trust betrayed.

Outrageous fortune
Turns her sling
Against his person,
And he the King!

Ah, in his throne room
Hangs so drear
Delusion's splendour,
Hiding—cold fear.

HEBEPHRENIA

The child in the sunlight dancing
Plays with the tenuous beams—
Life with stern step advancing
Breaks not her web of dreams.

Laughter, a silver fountain,
Leaps with her to the light—
Child of the mist-veiled mountain,
Know you not, it is night?

TRUE PARANOIA

Break, crested waves;
On the sheer cliff of onyx break
In wild foam—and fall back, powerless.

Lash, O wild winds,
'Gainst the unbending oak, aye, lash
In high fury—it is feelingless.

Beat, O deep drums,
Thunder your message fearsome—beat
Your dark rhythms—into soundlessness.

Speak, O strong Voice,
Speak peace, security—aye, speak!
Only You can fill this loneliness.

MANIC–DEPRESSIVE PSYCHOSIS

Jet
Of bright diamond spray
Play into the sunshine, yet
Scatter thy wanton jewels
Sky-
Reaching, yet returning ever
Thee-wards.
Say
'Midst thy bubbling laughter
That
Thou wouldst best
Forget.

What?
The slow-stirring stream—
Dream—
(Ruins in an abandoned lot
Spectre of slow and subtle death
Heath-
Stalking, yet returning ever
Thee-wards.)
Say,
'Midst thy muted sobbing
That
Thou wouldst best
Forget.

THE OTHERS

And then; "The Others"—all the endless range
Of body fighting soul; of age; of youth
Perpetuated in the smile of idiocy;
Of dark obsession; of urge uncontrolled,
Of the unnumbered twists of phantasy;
My sisters and my brethren are they all—
Familiar faces in this shadow'd land.

CROSSROADS

INSULIN SUB-SHOCK

The swift prick,
The smile, and the drawn shade.
Silence.
The long descent begins.
The winding stairway—
Dank and slippery stone,
Worn with the countless journeyings of dreams.
The slow drip
Of water seeping from a hidden spring.
The creak
Of unaccustomed hinges swinging wide—
Vista
Of an immensity of formless space—
A face
Featureless yet beautified beyond
A word-description—
Feet
Freed from a long-worn fetter.
Lightness—

Flung am I as an arrow to
Oblivion . . .

ELECTROSHOCK

Swift, subtle, servant's silent feet; which cross
Some velvet carpet with the firm, soft tread
Of one inheriting humility,
The while accustomed to omnipotence—
This is my servitor, all clad in light;
My servitor—and yet, my master, too . . .
Obedient to the trained and skilled hands
Of this or that young doctor—so I lie;
Constrained and arched; firm-gripped and motionless;
Un-gazing into concentrating eyes
Of earnest students—young themselves as I,
Now separated by the single word
"Insane!" from all that they consider . . . life.
The pulled switch brings the darkness, and the frail
Thin singing of a violin grows faint—
Then loud—my opening eyes look to the sun . . .

DANCE NIGHT

Smoke—
Lights, laughter, music,
Motion
(Paper ships
On an unbounded ocean)
Gaity—
Confusion—
Quality
Of fine illusion—
Balance—
Skill, swaying—
(Inward praying)
Goodbye, with laughter—
And after,
Back behind bars—
Stars
Witness to vows unspoken—
Dream's bauble
Shattered—
(Not that it mattered)
One moment's gladness—
Madness?
Even the blind
Find
Stars in the dirt—
Hurt?
Escape entrancing—
Dancing.

HALLUCINATION

This is the parting of the ways.
Here the road forks . . .
This way is mine;
And the road not taken—
Who can tell what lies
Down that mist-hidden path?
(Winding through desert lands
Over the barren hills, into infinity.)

Hush, do not speak so!
I have heard thee call
Down that strange echoing tunnel of half-light
I have seen thy form
(Silhouette, oh most elusive shadow!)
Against the glare at the dark hallway's end—
Approaching—
Retreating—
Between fluid walls
And floor and ceiling of half-molten glass.

This is the crossroads—
Here we take our leave;
Thou of me, oh speaking shadow,
I of thee . . .
Until what distant meeting by the sea?

UNREALITIES

Shadows—
  Silver sand—
    Stars—
Spiral of leaves—
  Autumn smoke . . .
    Steam . . .
      Dew . . .
Cob-webs—
  Chiffon . . .
    Satin . . .
      Water
Falling—
  Swirling . . .
    Curling . . .
      Purling . . .
Incense burning—
  Yearning . . .
    Turning . . .
      (Slowly, slowly)
Into strange
  Shapes—
    Apes . . .
      Drapes . . .
        Capes
And harbours, in what distant shore . . .
Oar dripping—
  Slipping . . .
    Slapping

Waves against the boat . . .
Oat
Tassels in the wind . . .
    Spindrift . . .
        Spray . . .
            Hay
Warm in the loft . . .
    Soft
        Coifed
Heads over Psalters
    Bent . . .
        Spent . . .
            Lent . . .
Coin of life—
    Strife . . .
        Knife—
Blue in the moonlight's
    Feel . . .
        Steal . . .
            Kneel . . .
                Real?
Under the wave . . .
    (Cave . . .
        Grave . . .)
            Lunge . . .
Over
    Over
        Oh . . .
            PLUNGE!

VOIX DE MYSTÈRE

And would you answer if I spoke?
And would you say
Something of peace? "Lady, I lay
My head against your hand."
Ah, do not draw away!
I cannot see you, for I am born blind.
Besides, the mists are binding, strangling me.
Do not reject me as the others did:
What I had hid
From them—my treasures—I would show to you;
And would you laugh, as I have heard you do
In some so-far-off valley of my dreams?
And if I followed your song-speaking,
Would you lead
Me to a land of laughter? For I need
Laughter instead of tears—
Or would it be
Instead, over the edge—into the sea?

CHANSON DU RÊVE

Flute
Note-showering, then mute
Muffled drums . . .
It comes—
The high clear singing of a hidden voice
Acquaint with fears,
Yet knowing to rejoice.
Violins,
Insidious harps and tinkling mandolins.
The deep-toned sobbing of the woodwinds—brass
Muting its clamour—O alas, alas
For the sad beauty of this song of dreams!
What then has vanished? It seems
To search for something—what is lost?
Is it beyond price and beyond cost?
And I, my voice with its soft keening blending,
Join to the dream my own search, never-ending.

PHANTASIE

Out of the swirling grey,
Colour—pastel half-tones
Deep'ning to throbbing hue—
Intensity . . .

Form, from the tenuous cloud
Sweeping with shivering speed
Into knife-edged outline—
Clarity . . .

And from the murmuring,
Sound, cacophony muffled,
Growing to crystal tone—
Purity . . .

Mist and a shifting pattern,
Voices—ah, symbol-folk!;
Light in a savage glow
Blinding me . . . suddenly,
Obscurity.

BALLET DE DÉMENCE

Tour jeté, pas de chat—
Ah—
Can you name the motion
Of the flowing,
Of the strange flower-like blowing
In the strong winds of emotion?
Mind and body reeling—
Appealing
To Beauty Infinite, to Law
Creative . . . destruction's leap-twist—
The death-throes of a dream—
And do they seem
Too much—and does the clenching of my fist
Fill you with fear and awe?
Fear—and can you name its name?
I have seen its face.
It is from this I flee . . .
Me—
This tossing leaf?
Beyond relief?
Wrath gives me grace . . .
As in a trance
I dance . . .

"A DONDE VAS?"

Whither
Now?

When?
How?

This . . . cease?
Peace?

Someone—
Aid?

Or; remain
Afraid?

Fear—
Near.

Mind—
Blind.

What next?
Sore-vex't

Heart saith—
Death.

Whither
Now?

PENDULUM-PULSE

This is the rhythm of my life—
The slow
Unhurried swinging of a pendulum,
Marking with fatal pulse the season's round.
The spring outside means nothing;
For, to me,
Fear like the winter snow has frozen my heart

And can it be that once again the hours,
Passing in cycle slow, will bring the flowers?
Or will Time's muffled drums beat out for me
A long death-march . . . into Eternity?

DESPAIR

Traveler, is there then
No last returning
From these distant plains?
Is that light burning
To call another home—not I?
And is this yearning
To be, like all the rest, unsatisfied?

Traveler, does the road
Have then no bending?
And to this waterless plain
Is there no ending?
No oasis of rest—am I
Then, but depending
On an illusion? I had rather I died.

Traveler, in this land
Is there no dying?
For death would taste so sweet—
And am I crying
Into a deafened ear? Oh I
Am sick of trying;
Yet there is one more thing I have not tried . . .
Suicide.

MOTIVE FOR SUICIDE

Only the dark
And a lone hound's baying—
The hunter's horn in the ancient call—
Sounds in the brush—
And hidden eyes watching—
A presence felt—a following footfall—

Wind in my face
And a cold rain falling—
Moan of the surf on the desolate shore—
Loneliness—Christ!
And a long trail's ending—
Mountains behind me—mist before—

Never a word—
Nor a kiss of friendship—
Never a sunrise—never a lark—
Never a dawn for my eyes to witness.
Only the dark.

PANIC

And is there anyone at all?
And is
There anyone at all?
I am knocking at the oaken door . . .
And will it open
Never now no more?
I am calling, calling to you—
Don't you hear?
And is there anyone
Near?
And does this empty silence have to be?
And is there no-one there at all
To answer me?

I do not know the road—
I fear to fall.
And is there anyone
At all?

RELAPSE

Up from the blackness
The hand—
So white—so fair
So choking-powerful—
Ah, I am bound!
Quick, struggle!
No—too late
I cannot make resistance—
Plunge—
Babel of voices—
Spiral into whirl
Of spinning colours—vortex, I—
Sky
Full of smashing stars—
Roar
Of the great cataract, to drown my scream.
Forgotten dreams
Flashing like fire before my misting eyes—
Help me, I fall!

"Miss, did you call?

The doctor's on his way—
Don't be afraid"—say—
Too late! I am prone—
Alone—alone—

IMPRESSIONS

WARD 8 DAYROOM

*(Written while listening to a Disc Jockey's program,
in a "disturbed" ward)*

In a subway far from Ireland,
Far, far away,
Far far away,
(And how far away can you be?
Don't ask me.)

Round and round and round she goes,
And where she stops,
Damned if I know.
(Or care.)

Kiss me once and kiss me twice—
It's been a long, long time,
And you'd be so nice to come home to—
(But I would prefer you
With shoes on and a Toni.)

And, Oh, yes Lawd, nobody knows
The trouble I see . . .
(Anything *but*,
Hallelujah!)
It's Spring again and birds on the wing again start to
  sing again—
Well, don't they always?

Hey, Momma,
I got a trauma—
SHOW ME THE WAY TO GO HOME!

STRONG-ROOM

O beautiful rigidity of steel
Bars—fair solidity of walls,
Concrete, so real in its
Stark purity—
Oak of a double-locked door—
Tree now no more
Yet budding leaves for me—
Security!

No need to strip me, shut me from the world;
Naked and helpless runs my soul,
Stripped of the fripperies of vanity.
And prisoned far more sure
(Can I endure
It?) am I by what must be
Insanity!

PSYCHIATRIST

Voyager, what seas,
What oceans have you sailed?
And what strange shores,
Cliff-guarded, ringed with foam,
And inaccessible, have you set foot upon?
Into what quiet bays
And through what seething maelstroms has your craft
Ventured its way; and what the Polar Star
For your phantastic navigation?

Oh the wind is strong
At sea—and piercing to the heart the cry
The stricken sea-hawks give before they die . . .
And he who dares the wildly rolling wave,
The savage spray, must then indeed be brave—

O conqueror of the sea—
Canst conquer me?

PSYCHOTHERAPY

Pulse
Behind closed lids
Beating as wings beat
Vainly against bars . . .

Words—
A scattered heap
Pouring
As coins pour
From a secret hoard . . .

Tears—
A silent stream
Flowing
As Lethe flows
In the vale of dreams.

Adventurer—
Walk watchfully here
Treading
As pilgrims tread
Through an uncharted land.

A hand
On a long-closed door
Opening—
Beyond what lies?
Skies!

GROUP THERAPY

Traveler, what port?
What? Yes, I too!
I'll along with you—
The night is dark—here is my hand, good friend.

And are we near the end?
I'm weary; have you bread to share?
There. Where
Is your home? You have none? Nor have I.

The sky
Feels cloudy—it will storm.
Here is my pilgrim's cloak to keep you warm.
And shall we reach the land?

It is so hard to understand
The ways of vision, so I find—
What? You, too,—
Blind?

HYDROTHERAPY

Chill!!
Lie still
(Intricacy of wrapped cocoon)
Soon
Sleep.
Yes, weep;
Lying as the dead lie——form
Warm
(Heat
Of the shattered heart's last beat)
Tremble
At the immensity of symbol—
Chain
Fetters of iron unseen—the brain
Close-
Prisoned—the spirit comatose.
The shape
Of the long coffin—last escape—
On what warm breast
Rest?
Then
With the finality of an "Amen"
Strong hands and supple set you free—
Me?
Release . . .
Peace?

EBB–TIDE

FREEDOM

When I was free
I walked the streets alone—
Faces and feet flowed past
Going where? Being who?
And nobody knew at all—
Nobody cared—
Each in his little shell of self
Listened to his private sea—
Listened to his own mind's chatter,
Forgetting me . . .

Now behind bars
Earth and the heavens are mine—
Life in uneasy whirl slips past
Going where? Being who?
Though nobody knows at all,
Though nobody cares,
No little shells of self
Block out the sea—
Minds that have ceased to chatter
Remember me . . . . .

This was not so
When I was free.

WISH

My wish
Is not now for my freedom
Nor for sanity—
Not to be once more
Whole and clean again,
Free from that which lurks
Far, deep, inside my brain—

Nor wit
Nor smooth sophistication
Nor urbanity—
Nor to control bright words,
Showered like silver stars,
Singing as the birds
Even behind these bars.

My wish
Is but to tell my story
To humanity—
To let them know that God
(Yes, and in spite of Freud!)
Lives closer to the minds
Whose self-shields are destroyed.

My wish
Is for His love,
Even in insanity.

EPISODE

With the finality of block on weft
Driving the taut thread home,
Let it be ended;
Into the careful pattern, dark and light,
Of the past's weaving; so
Let it be blended—

O the bright thread, dyed fair
In the sharp hues of pain—
Keen silver of tears, and cramoisie
Of mine own blood, shed in an agony—
Sever from it the plain
Dark-tinted winding that sustained it, ye
Shears of the Fates! For those drab shades oppress;

And let the tapestry end in these frayed edges—Let
The pattern slip now into formlessness.

ALTAR

(Resignation to a Loss)

Fold away the still-unspotted linens,
Cast out the withered and unscented flowers,
Cover in black the dull and lustreless gold,
And rob the guttering candles of their last
Pale flame. The sacrifice is made,
What had to be has been—
And now, no more—
(Ciboria tarnished . . . O'er the empty pews
The silent Crucified looks into nothingness.)

The pendant sword descended has to sever
The silver cord—forever and for ever . . .
Is there one bell to toll?
"Never . . . ever . . .
Never . . .
Never . . ."

EDGE

Here the sea stops, and knocks imperiously,
Urgently at the shore
Heaving black shoulders up against the door.
The low winds mutter in the sodden sedge—
One step more from this storm-battered ledge
And I am part of wave and crest and foam—
They are knocking for me now,
"Come home! Come home!"

EBB-TIDE

One Polar Star
In a most empty and unpitying sky.
One fisher's song, that swells only to die
Into unbroken silence.
And the long reach
Of the sea's fingers clutching at the beach—
Ah! The relentless tide is drawing me
Over the border—into infinity.

JEREMIAD

DE PROFUNDIS

The final word
The *"Consummatum est."*
It is finished, over, done,
"Ich kann nicht mehr."
What I have done, is done.
The sails are set,
And, beating out to sea—
The Finis-terre behind us fades in fog.
Horizon—in shadow;
Grey seas, and greyer skies.
Menace.
"Ich kann nicht mehr."
This is the final gesture,
After this—what is done
Is not of me.
I can no more.
I am too tired of vainly struggling—
Of swimming through an endless sea of glue;
Of slogging through
Quicksand—to what lost terra firma
I shall go down—
Yes, go down in the dark—
Ah, bitterness!
Defeat is gall and wormwood to my tongue—
And yet—
"Ich kann nicht mehr."
Here is the broken sword—

And here the harp that shall not sing again
Of brave endeavor.
"Eloi! Eloi!"
Out of the depths
I have cried to Thee ...

TENEBRAE

"O vos omnes
Qui transitis per viam
Attendite et videte
Si est dolor
Sicut dolor meus . . ."

For the waters have indeed
Come unto my soul.
And not the wildly fair
Tumultuous singing cataracts of spring . . .
No, nor the leaping, lashing, foam-head waves
Of the unconquered ocean;
No, nor yet
The grandeur of the rivers to the sea . . .
The waveless lake—the everflowing spring . . .
The rock-battalioned gem of deep-sea pool . . .
No—but the dark and slowly-rolling tides
Foamless and silent—deadly still and cold,
Of that vast ocean without bound . . .
Despair.

For; "I am the man
Who see my poverty
By the rod of His indignation . . .
He has led me into darkness,
And not into light . . .

Attendite, et videte
Si est dolor sicut dolor meus."

MISERERE

"*Miserere nobis, Domine—parce nobis—*"
(Fragments
Of what was beautiful,
Grime-sodden,
Scatter the baked earth—
Bed
Of the soft-running stream
Parched—sere-leaved trees
Rustle with weary sigh
Of a half-hearted breeze.)

"*Quomodo sedet
Sola,
Civitas plena populo—
Plorans ploravit
In nocte—
Non est
Qui consoletur eam . . .*"

My heart hath expected
Reproach and misery . . .

O let this chalice pass . . .

"Miserere nobis, Domine
Miserere nobis . . ."
For I live not, now,
Nor doth Christ live in me.

"De multitudine misericordiae tuae
Miserere nobis . . ."

NUNC DIMITTIS

"Cui comparabo te
Vel cui assimilabo te
O virgo filia Jerusalem?
Magna est
Enim velut mare
Contritio tua."

Now is the wheel at rest,
The silver cord
Is cut,
The golden bowl is broken—
The pitcher
Goes not to the polluted well.

Now is the beginning
(*Incipit lamentatio prophetae.*)
Of a last song.
Now is the hour of
Which was written
In the seven-sealed book,

"Quando coeli movendi sunt
Et terra
Dum veneris judicare saeculum
Per ignem."

Now dost Thou dismiss Thy servant
O Lord, according to Thy word—
But not—
No, never more—
In peace.

LIBERA ME

"Dies illa, dies irae
Calamitatis et miseriae;
Dies, magna
Et amara valde . . ."

Iron is cold in the winter's air
And blood in the raw wound springs anew
At the chilled manacles' chafe. And feet
Move deathly slow along the upward path.
Ah—is there no crest to this long hill?
Or at the end,—is there only—the Cross?

"Tremens facta sum ego
Et timeo . . ."

Deliver me, O Lord
From eternal death,
In that tremendous day
When Thou shalt come to judge
The earth by fire.

ALTER CHRISTUS

Lord, for the pain I cursed You for last night
I do most gladly offer thanks today . . .
For, not with pride but deep humility
In me, and by me, and through me, I find—You!
In my stripped loneliness, Your own imprisonment—
My bruises mark Your scourging; and the same
Rude jests ring in my ears that rang in Yours—
And round my aching head I seem to feel
Even today, the racking crown of thorns . . .
I too was bound—and, though I never died,
I was like You—my *spirit* crucified.

CURTAIN

ASH WEDNESDAY

"Memento homo, quia pulvis es ..."
But for the signed, the sealed, the set-apart,
No symbol-ash is needed. On their brows
Is written, clearer far, their frailty.
Torn by eroding waves and blasting winds
Little by little, crumbles the strongest rock
Into a pile of dust; and thus the spirit
Crumbles beneath too much adversity.
Yet, from the burned-out clinker of these lives
Warmth has not wholly vanished—after Lent
The Resurrection brings the sun again.
O pyre of consummation! Cleansing flame!
Out of the ashes of this seeming ruin
Let us rise Phoenix-like, reborn in pain!

GOOD FRIDAY

"My people, what have I done?
In what have I offended thee?
Answer me . . ."

Up the hushed aisle in the three prostrations
The faithful move. In the stripped sanctuary
The black-garbed priests sing slowly.

"Agios o Theos
Agios ischyros
Agios athanatos
Eleison imas."

But I? I
Am not there this year
To see.
What need?
For I
Am likewise crucified
On what invisible
Calvary?

REJECTION

Oh, to a deafened ear I sang my songs
The fairest that I knew, my songs of love—
Oh, for a blinded eye I painted scenes
Of Paradise, in colours from my bright
Soul-rainbow of emotions! And I gave
To a rejecting hand my priceless treasures;
My pearl of infinite price—my gold—my heart.
I brought the fire stolen from the gods
To warm a heart of ice—
There is no need
In me to reconsider suicide
Because of you, a part of me has died.

FEAR

How often in the old tales,
(Strange sagas, worn by retelling
Into an almost mystic age-shrouded
    pattern),
Have I found the story of the princess
    shocking
The rigid formality of the court,
The settled ploddings of her people—
And probably herself as well—by
    leading
On a silver chain,
The tamed steel and black velvet anger
Of a panther, at her heels.

And now I, too,
Though by no means a princess,
Lead on a slender, all-too-fragile chain
(All too fragile, indeed,
For the hot, hard flame of its forging)
Just such a jungle power as she of
    long ago

I hear the step,
The muffled tread behind me;
I know the rippling of hard sinews
Beneath the soft midnight pelt;
And, too, I know
What others cannot see;
That in those cold jade eyes
Smoulders a spark soon whipped to
    sudden flame;
That in those velvet following feet
The long claws lie light-sheathed,
    ready for the spring.

BEYOND THIS HILL

Beyond this hill, what had I thought to find
But green and pleasant plains, a quiet stream,
And spreading trees to shade a traveler's rest?
The road I came leads long and devious
Through the strange folkless countries of the mind,
Whence having come, one never may return;
Now, I had thought to find some brighter land—
But through the mists swirled from yon stagnant pool
I see a treeless desert vale beyond,
Wherein who asks for bread finds but a stone.

PRECIPICE ✕

This is the end of the song—
This is the close of the tale—
The final curtain—
  Only the silence now.
  Only the empty shell—
  The barriered door.

This is the edge of the cliff—
This is the end of the road—
Void space before—
  Only the darkness behind,
  Only the blackness below—
  There is no more.

This the long-gathering force
None can resist—
This is the armored fist
Hurling you down . . .

UNDERSCORING

It is an old, tattered and quite passé
Piece of a manuscript—
The childish scrawl
Of the first chapters touches maturity
And then, the crab-like scratchings that a man
Makes when his mind, his body, and his heart
Are racked and racked again with agony.
O reader, scan this last and final page,
And mark you well the crimson underscoring;
For these are written in my own heart's blood . . .
Remorse, despair, and fear, and loneliness;
And ah! the final cruel cut of loss . . .
Reader, the cry I write has echoed down
From Christ Himself, dictating from the Cross!